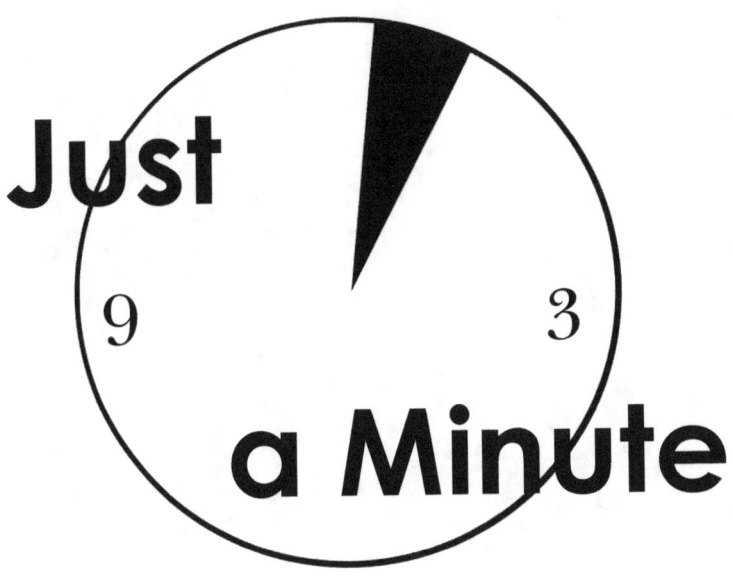

Just

a Minute

Short, mostly humorous,
mini-articles about life's little
adventures

Betty J. O'Brien

ISBN: 1456352512
ISBN-13: 9781456352516

Acknowledgment

To my treasured editors, Carol Davis, Sharon
Ibrahim, and Carol Swanke.

Table of Contents

A Toast To The New Year

Curtain Up!
The New Year's on the set,
Before it makes its exit,
May all our goals be met.

It's About Time

I don't worry about time as much as I used to, and I feel good about it. I was always on time or early for appointments, so I have a healthy respect for other people's time as well as my own. My alarm used to tell me when to wake up and get my show on the road. Now I wake up, stretch, and luxuriate because I have little idea what time it is, and don't care. I think of a clock less as a crisp geometric circle and more like artist Salvador Dali's elongated, lounging clock.

I have attacked thoughts of time with a vengeance. I will not boil a 3-minute egg, make a soufflé, or serve Baked Alaska for dessert. The egg might be overcooked, the soufflé might fall flat and the Baked Alaska might melt before I could get it to the table. A bowl of cold cereal, a casserole and a cookie is much less taxing.

I don't plant day lilies, night blooming jasmine, or Four O'clock bushes either. I can look at petunias, marigolds, or roses mid-day or midnight, they don't care and neither do I.

Season tickets and library books are other threats I won't tolerate. I'd rather pay more for a single performance I want to see right now than guess that I may be available on the scheduled date six months from now. Also, I'd rather buy used books, borrow books from friends or just watch the movie than fret about the countdown of days I have left to finish or renew a book at the library.

It's a little risky, but I don't pay much attention to expiration dates. My theory is, if it works, as in medicine, tastes good, as in food, it's probably healthful, not harmful. I will not be intimidated by expiration dates. The only expiration date I'm really concerned about is my own. God only knows when that will be and that's OK with me.

Sneaky Senior Secrets

My daughter called and asked if I'd like to go with the family to Disneyland. "There's plenty of room in the van." I sighed wearily and said, "I'm a little tired today; I think I'll just stay home and rest." I snapped the cell phone shut, put on my gardening clogs, went outside and planted 49 pansies and mulched 10 Podocarpus trees.

About a week ago, my son told me that he and his wife were going up to the Santa Rosa Plateau to hike a few trails. "Want to come along?" "No," I said, "I've got this nasty bunion just behind my left big toe, so I'd better not go – I'd just slow you down." I then snugged into my custom-fitted running shoes, went down to the Clubhouse and ran three miles on the treadmill in the air conditioned exercise room while I watched TV.

I do feel guilty about these amendments to the truth, but not guilty enough to stop. For instance, friends asked me to join them for the sumptuous Sunday Brunch at their country club last Sunday. I said, "Gee, that sounds wonderful, but my stomach is a little queasy this morning, so I'll pass, but thanks." I went to the kitchen, had a bowl of cottage cheese with fresh ground black pepper and cut up sweet pickle, and a blueberry Danish along with a side of sliced pickled beets. I did miss the champagne, though.

Last Christmas, a friend I worked with for many years called, saying excitedly, "I've got two free tickets to *The Nutcracker,* good sound system, great seats. Want to go?" I sighed (I'm good at sighs). "I've seen the Nutcracker so many times I feel impelled to get up and leave when the bear dances. Please choose someone who would appreciate the production." In truth, I saw *The Nutcracker* once and vowed never to see the sappy thing again.

When I look in a good mirror and the image is not usually great, it's kind of flattering when a person asks, "Is your hair naturally curly?" I say, "Yes." What I mean is, naturally it's curly because my stylist has designed it that way with a good perm and constant upkeep for the last ten years.

And speaking of looks, I also like it when I breeze into a meeting on a sharp, cold January day and someone invariably asks, "Aren't you cold?" "No," I say, "Good red blood and super circulation, I guess." Actually, my crewneck top with elastic cuffed sleeves and light sweat pants and socks hide lace-trimmed toasty silk thermal underwear.

Finally, now I'll tell you a REAL secret. There really is a Senior Advantage. I'm workin' it.

Beef Stew for One

I get the boneless chuck roast out of the refrigerator and begin to cut it into cubes. One child takes fresh carrots out of the hydrator, twists off the lacy green tasseled tops and begins peeling swiftly. Soon a pile of thin orange carrot confetti builds in the sink. Another child deftly turns rough brown potatoes, paring to reveal the white, firm flesh beneath. I brown the cubed meat in hot olive oil and add pungent, weeping chunks of onion. The knife cutting through carrots and potatoes sounds like galoshes on new snow. We compare our work keeping all pieces about the same size, and then dump the vegetables into the pot. Later I watch the hot rivulets gather on the dome of the Dutch oven and slide back into the stew. I carefully lift the hot, heavy, lid and release the smell of home into the kitchen.

Now, I make beef stew for one. It keeps my body healthy and my memories strong.

Valentine

A White cross on red denotes something Swiss,
A Red cross on white says something's amiss,
But a red heart on white with verses so fine
Can only mean you,
Must be my Valentine.

Unsportsmanlike Conduct

Almost all of my dentists have had bad knees or knee replacements because of football injuries. I'm glad football was mainly a male's game when I was in school. I think I have pretty good knees because I didn't go out for football. I don't have tennis elbow either. I've used elbow grease to clean sinks but never raised a racquet on a tennis court. Speaking of sports that involve balls makes me think of baseball. Those fancy "round-up" maneuvers by baseball pitchers cause rotator cuff injuries. My shoulders are fine. The only thing I pitch is an occasional fit.

I don't move fast, or a lot. But marathon runners get shin splints. While watching TV I've seen them writhe in pain on the track. Makes me glad all I run is water. That reminds me, I don't get swimmers ear either. Those three minute showers don't imperil my mostly dry ears.

I understand there are some female boxers. No way would I risk a concussion, even in the Feather Weight Division. I also understand turf toe can keep a high-priced NFL star out from under the dome for weeks. Worst toe injury I've had is an ingrown toenail. Not fun but not career threatening either.

It may be unsportsmanlike conduct, but I'm heading for the sofa. I know I'm risking keester cankers or butt bunions, but I'll take my chances.

Surprises

I don't know the origin of the word "surprise," but I do know that it means something unexpected, and not always good, is about to happen.

One of my first surprises was at the neighborhood candy store. When I had a rare nickel to spend, I would look through the rounded glass front of the display counter and say, "That one, the green one with the balloons on it." Surprises were heavily wrapped opaque paper packages about the size and shape of a hot dog on a bun that hid the contents. One could rattle the precious treat and guess what its contents might be. There would always be a small toy, maybe a tin ring or a shell, which would open under water to reveal a paper flower on a string, a piece of gum and possibly some small hard candies. Most of my very young surprises were happy ones.

Happy surprises were not limited to childhood though. Once I eagerly scanned the street in front of the library hoping for a metered spot right out front. And there it was; snug but possible I thought. I swung the car into the short spot at one try, and got out of the car to gather an armload of books to carry up the steps and across the deep lawn to the library doors. I nodded to a man sitting on the high retaining wall swinging his legs and eating his lunch. As he took a bite of his sandwich, he said, "Lady, I never thought you'd get that car in there." More recently, my sister and I were putting a 6 ft. fake Ficus tree I'd just bought into our Honda Civic, when we eyed a security vehicle stopped near us. He said, "I want to see you two put that tree in that little car." We said, "Watch." I crawled into the back seat, unlocked the seat back and lowered it flat. My sister pushed the pot through to me and I snugged it up against the back of the front seat. The tree easily fit into the car. The guard laughed and waved good-bye.

I also remember a bad surprise; or maybe it was really a good-bad surprise. I had applied for and interviewed for a three-week summer teaching job. Leaving town for a few days, I confidently gave my Department Chair a phone number where I could be reached. The call never came; I didn't get the job. I was so depressed, my supervisor said, "I'm only telling you this because you are unreasonably troubled by this rejection. You never had a chance; the person was selected before you applied." The bad surprise; I didn't get the job. The good surprise; it had nothing to do with my qualifications.

Remember little Ronnie Howard, now a famous Hollywood producer and director, who as a child in The Music Man sang about the Wells

Fargo Wagon, with his adorable lisp? As he sees the Wells Fargo wagon coming down the street he sings, "....There could be something thspecial, really thspecial, just for me." I believe it with all my heart.

My Junk Drawer

I decided to clean out the junk drawer in the kitchen today. I lifted the drawer off its track and discovered the reason it hasn't closed properly for years. Crunched in the back of the drawer was a birth announcement. The child is now twenty years old and in college. I picked up two tall, slim golf tees, one yellow and one green; there was no advertizing. I playfully imagined they could be for golfers with bad backs. There were 4 jar openers, one in the original sealed plastic package. All for companies no longer in existence. Next I stirred a passel of keys and looked for some identifying marks. One had a metal banded cardboard disc that said, "St.Pat. P.J." I gasped, that was my son's locker key from the fifth grade at St. Patrick's elementary school. He's married now and has two sons in high school. There were two swizzle sticks, one said PSA, and one said AirCal. Both airlines are now extinct. Next I found a purple tong, the spoon half. I guess I frugally thought I'd use the good half after the fork half broke. I next picked up 3 mechanical can openers. Out with them. Anything an electric can opener doesn't open I don't eat. I spied a very fancy winged wine bottle opener. Spent a lot of money for the thing but always did find it too threatening to use. Next I picked up two strange items. Momentarily puzzled, I then remembered they were gadgets to make melon balls. I haven't made melon balls for so long I think I've lost the knack. I don't plan to relearn the skill.

Wearily I wiped up petrified crumbs with a soft hot dishcloth and replaced the drawer. Tomorrow, or the next day, or at lease very SOON I'll clean the other half of the drawer.

Designer Complaints

Psychiatrists and therapists will listen to me complain; they call it "venting" and charge a lot of money. Complaining does make me feel better, so I've developed a private stash of what I call "Designer Complaints." For example, when my feet hurt I know it's because I wear pretty, but ill-fitting, sandals all day. But I tell myself, "You've got to stop wearing stiletto heels and dancing all night." Somehow, it helps.

When I'm fatigued, I know it's because I've carried around a few too many pounds for a few too many years, but I lecture myself, "You've got to give up power walking, stretch aerobics or Pilates and you won't feel so tired." When I dive for antacids, I know it's because an hour ago I had a big fried fast food dinner, but I pretend I had a second helping of Lobster Newburg which caused my discomfort.

Still on food, I'm not about to tell anyone I have designer dentistry. I have more crowns than the Queen of England. But I quietly choose never to order tough steak or al dente vegetables – or eat peanut brittle. The very word "crunchy" sets my teeth on edge.

I have handy but top secret "designer tools" to open, twist, or pry things I used to manage easily. I even have "angel wings" on my faucets. A gentle push or pull controls the water's flow. No complaints about failing strength cross my lips.

I even have a recurring designer dream. I go to the doctor who says, "You need a face lift. It will help you hear better, see better and breathe better. All covered by your insurance, of course."

Finally, my favorite complaint was not designed by me. Long ago, I asked my small daughter, ill with a miserable cold and fever, how she felt. She replied, "Just a little bit fine." Now that's a classy complaint.

Happy St. Patrick's Day

He was there beneath the Nutmeg gate,
Upon my soul I swear it,
A green top hat was on his head,
So small I couldn't wear it.

He clutched a pot that flashed of gold,
His eyes ablaze, his cheeks acrinkle,
"Share?" I asked. "No." I was told,
And he vanished in a twinkle

Woodworking

I vividly remember tip-toeing through the dining room as my father, yet again shellacked the oak double pedestal table he'd made. He would raise his left hand, shiny paintbrush in his right hand, and say, "Go slowly, don't raise any dust till this dries." Although a machinist for U.S. Steel, he'd made many pieces of furniture. There were, as well as the table, four chairs, two upholstered vanity benches, a tall cigarette stand, and a tabouret, that I know about.

The slim two shelved cigarette stand was beside the grey leather recliner in the living room. The top shelf held a big glass ashtray and his pipe. The second shelf held only the giant red can of Prince Albert smoking tobacco. After work, and often after dislodging tiny steel filings from his fingers with a needle, he would settle into the recliner with his pipe and read the Saturday Evening Post. The tabouret, a graceful small cabinet stood to the right of the front door as you entered the house. It had wide, deep dark wood pockets on each side to hold magazines. Between the magazine pockets was a storage area with two small doors. The door pulls were slender brass trumpets which tap-tapped each time I dusted the tabouret.

I learned an appreciation for well tended wood but never actually saw my father make a piece of furniture. I did see my grandfather at work. I would sit half way down the cellar steps, just about level with the high wattage unshaded bulb dangling from the ceiling. While licking my butter pecan ice cream cone, I watched sawdust fly and smelled the fragrant pine as my grandfather bent over the piece he worked on, heedless of the chips gathering on his polished high top blackshoes.

Until I met my neighbor, a woodworking teacher, many years later, I'd forgotten those pleasant times with wood. He was making a third cedar chest and knew exactly what he wanted. When an infrequent order of cedar came in to the local lumberyard, he was invited to come in and choose the best pieces. He totally disdained the highly advertised cedar chests for new brides as cheap veneered and shoddily made pieces. On Saturday mornings when he could work on his own projects, I often went with him, to watch and carefully sweep the cedar shavings into bags to put in my bureau drawers and closets.

One day he said, "Want to help?" and handed me a big flat shop pencil. "Sure," I said. "Climb in the cedar box and draw a line so I know where to place the piano hinges." I climbed into the cedar box, he put the lid on and in the dark chest I made the proper marks.

Recently, I helped my sister settle the estate of a long-time friend of almost 99 years. Most decisions about her possessions were routine and easy, except for the teacart. She had inherited it long ago. It was at least a hundred years old. This beautiful piece shimmered in the morning sunlight. An appraiser was due any minute. I stroked its lustrous surface and felt again the wonder of wood.

The Toddler Principle

There's nothing so terrible about the "terrible twos," especially when you are two. If you don't make it to the potty, so what, if you no longer love the spaghettios you have loved for two weeks straight, so what, if you say loudly to your parent, who is patiently standing in the supermarket line, "That lady is fat," so what. If you say "NO," when you actually mean "YES," so what.

The worst thing about being a terrible two is that it only lasts about a year. You will never enjoy the freedom of expression you do now. Nasty remarks will warrant a smack on the butt, tantrums and tirades will be out maneuvered by seasoned elders. All too soon you will be pushed and shoved into the mold society has prepared for you. Gone are those halcyon days when you could play with your food, splash through puddles in your new shoes, sink your face into a birthday cake and say no to anything, and often. Society erodes this free spirited way of life soon enough. We learn to act "appropriately," say "please" and "thank you," and do as we're told all too soon.

So here is The Toddler Principle: Act when you really care, play with your food and say "NO" a lot.

The Oiler

I like to oil things. Maybe it's psychological; I like things to run smoothly. The screech of metal on metal arouses the passion in me to fix it. Oiling doesn't take a lot of physical strength to perform. That particularly fits my rather puny physique. It makes me feel so powerful to arrest destructive friction.

This passion can cause family problems. Just after my oldest son was married I visited him and his wife in their Chicago apartment. The stove knobs were grimy and hard to turn, so I pulled them off, washed them, oiled them and replaced them. Next I noticed that the closet door in their bedroom moved sluggishly. I inspected the track and found it full of dust. I cleaned the track and applied the treasured oil.

When my son and his wife returned that night I expected accolades. Before I could explain my improvements, I heard BLAM from the bedroom where my son had changed clothes and closed the closet door. "MOM!" he howled.

Uh, oh, The Oiler had struck again.

Spring Roll Call

Jack in the Pulpit,
Lily of the Nile,
Queen Anne's Lace and Roses,
Winter's face their names displace,
And classy spring exposes.

Gardening, Anyone?

I picked off a small perfect impatiens blossom and brought it inside to look at more closely under my magnifier. I adjusted the lens and there, looking back at me, was a small, very green, worm. I shuddered, squished it in several tissues and went back to work spreading fragrant, shredded cedar under the shrubs. Suddenly, a sharp cedar splinter came right through my heavy gardening glove and into my finger. I removed the splinter with tweezers and treated the painful area. When I returned to the yard, I noticed that the color bowls needed water and hurried to shower them. Alas, I had forgotten to put on gardening shoes and splashed my nearly new white sneakers with dirty water.

Earlier I had cut roses and put them on the kitchen counter. When I returned to them, I discovered that a slimy snail had crawled out of the roses and into the sink. I flicked it into the drain and vengefully snapped on the disposal. inspected, trimmed and arranged the roses, then went back outside to fill the big fountain's bowl. The heavy scent of jasmine lay on the still air. I leaned on the hot wrought iron fence and waited for the bowl to fill. Just then, beyond the fence, a small crew of gardeners mowed, edged and trimmed vigorously in the hot sun. I turned off the hose and ran into the house.

Gotta' get those guys some cold lemonade.

Clean Up! Paint Up! Plant Up!

It was April when the Art teacher wrote those words on the blackboard. (It WAS a blackboard then.) Next, while placing big white pieces of poster board on each desk she said, "Create a poster. Construction paper, scissors, paste, etc. are on the side table under the windows." Each April since then, I feel the urge to clean, paint, and plant.

This April, I cleaned the gutters. Well, not really, but I did hold open the extra-strength Hefty bag for my helper to drop muddy dirt into it I also pointed out a few two or three inch baby weeds visible against the red roof tiles. Next I cleaned the tracks of the big mirror doors in the bathroom. Down on my hands and knees, I pushed along wet Q-tips to clear the tracks of dust. Then with fresh Q-tips, sprayed with WD40, I treated the tracks. This took a lot of Q-tips but the result was worth it. Then I cleaned out the medicine cabinet. Who needs three pill splitters? I tested all three with expired aspirin tablets and kept the best one; also threw out the expired aspirin. I'd like to clean the key holes in the compartments for large packages under the bank of mailboxes, but fear this might be illegal.

So much for cleaning. Next, came painting. I didn't actually paint, but I did supervise. I followed along as the painter transformed the dull, weathered wrought iron fence to fresh, glossy black. I snipped off accidentally painted Hawthorn bush leaves. Then he painted the little bistro set outside the front door. I sat there on my little Rubbermaid stool and gently pointed out a couple curly-cues he'd missed. "Lady, I think I hear your phone ringing," the painter said. I don't think the phone was ringing, but I picked up my stool and left anyway.

So, now it was on to planting. I know planting, so that was the easiest. I love spring bulbs, but gave up their proper care and storage after a bunch of them sprouted, rotted, and died on the garage shelf. Now I enjoy the flowers and turn over the residual mess to my daughter. Next I placed nursery-planted color bowls around the patio, carefully testing the clever little watering device in each one.

That's it. CLEAN UP! PAINT UP! PLANT UP! I'm through again for another year. I'm exhausted. Will somebody bring me a glass of lemonade while I lounge here and survey my handiwork?

Childhood Revisited

If this is my second childhood, in many ways it's better than the first. Childhood is highly overrated. For me, it was one big worry after another. First school hit me. Rain or snow, hot or cold – out into the world I went. It was a lot more hectic than home. I had to talk when I wanted to be quiet and be quiet when I wanted to talk.

Maybe poet Robert Browning got it right when he said, "Grow old along with me! The best is yet to be..." If the highs of youth are not as high, the lows of adulthood are not as low.

As we age, I think we become more able to accentuate our positives and tolerate our negatives. Poet Emily Dickinson was put in a closet as a child and told to "be still." My theory is that she was a constant chatterbox, to the dismay of her weary parents. Maybe, in that dark closet, she began to develop her skills as a writer and poet. She had to think rather than talk, and then later put those thoughts on paper. Generations of readers continue to enjoy her prolific writings, but when she writes things like "Hope is a thing with feathers," I confess I'm no big fan of hers.

Another theory I have is that when we mature adults are labeled "cantankerous or cranky," we are just not willing to be what family, friends and society want us to be. Maturity is freeing. We can, much more often, eat what we want to eat, go where we want to go and enjoy the company of those whose company we enjoy.

Now, in reasonably good health and with considerable leisure time, I reflect with joy and revise past decisions with confidence to make my life the best that it can be right now. Yes, I think Browning had it right when he said, "Grow old along with me! The best is yet to be..."

I'm working on it.

Sunbelt April Showers

Rain drums upon the skylight,
Rain courses through the creek,
Wide awake or dreaming,
It's an April rain I seek.

A Matter of Perspective

Early in the morning on a hot July day, we were ascending the Grapevine on our way south to Disneyland when my six-year-old daughter leaned over the front seat of the station wagon. "Mom," she whispered, as her bag of Fruit Loops spilled into my lap, "look at the golden trees." I saw the hot east rising sun on bare black saplings on a high hillside to our right. I shifted my perspective, and I too saw the golden trees.

Once, strolling down the curved brick walkway to our summer cottage, I spied gardeners viciously yanking clumps of clover out of the shiny, damp green lawn. Hurrying to get out of their way so they could clear the scruffy walkway, I looked down and saw a large perfect four leaf clover silhouetted against a rain-washed red brick. I carefully picked it and stored it in my little blue fake leather covered diary until it disintegrated. Again, a matter of perspective; debris to the gardeners, treasure to me.

Another time, my young daughters were crouched over a big Kleenex box between them on the floor. They were busily creating miniature furniture for their collection of tiny plastic people. I observed and said, "You left one Kleenex in the box, "No," they said, that's the wall-to-wall carpeting."

Several years ago, in an unfamiliar department store, I approached a tall, slim young woman at the cosmetics counter and asked, "Can you tell me where the Petite Department is? "Sure," she said, "over there where the short racks are." Crossing the floor, I spotted a chic suit I liked. Getting out my credit card, I said to myself, "Hmm, the racks don't look short to me."

Shakespeare said it in *Love's Labor Lost,* and Ben Franklin said it about a century later. "Beauty is in the eye of the beholder," or you could say it's a matter of perspective.

Things I Don't Like

I've been around long enough to know there are things I don't like. To start with, I don't like the adjectives "cantankerous," "crotchety," or "cranky," but they probably fit.

There are other things I don't like. I don't like any sort of sprinkles on good ice cream, or strappy sandals on people with bumpy feet. I don't like sycamore trees, because they are the last to get leaves in the spring and first to lose them in the fall. I don't like trite expressions like "cold as ice," "hot as fire," or "quick as a wink." I don't like anything "zany" describes. I have no taste for cold soups, even if they have fancy French or Spanish names. I don't like "cutesy" euphemisms, like "previously owned" for used cars or "anti-aging treatment" for wrinkle cream. I don't like perky people when I'm enjoying a perfectly good, bad mood day. I don't like "new and improved" anything; it's usually not, and costs more.

I feel better now. Have a nice day....or not.

My Sophomore Prom – The Gift of Love

We were reading "A Midsummer Night's Dream" in Miss Haggardy's English class one late spring morning, when the phone rang. Miss Haggartey turned and said, "Betty, you are wanted in Mr. Fife's office immediately." The whole class went, "OOOOO." Mr. Fife was the Assistant Principal and much feared disciplinarian. As I left the classroom I scoured my soul for any possible offense I'd committed. None came to mind.

I entered Mr. Fife's office. He succinctly said, "You are to meet your mother downtown, as soon as possible, at the dress shop next to the Cinderella shoe store." He smiled. I said "Thank you," and left his office.

I walked down the hill, boarded the bus for downtown Pittsburgh and dropped my nickel in the token box. During the short ride I thought about how unusual it was for my mother to go out of the house alone. Almost always, my father, my sister or I accompanied her. She was very uncomfortable about being alone away from home.

I walked into the shop and there she was with a long yellow dress over her arm. "Betty," she said, "you need to try on this dress because the sale is final. There is a black streak on the skirt, but I think I can get it out."

I slipped the gown over my head and my mother ran up the zipper. I turned to look at my image in the full length mirror and gasped with pleasure. Over the bright yellow satin A-line skirt was an overskirt of pale yellow organdy, on which were scattered bunches of tiny appliqued yellow blue and red flowers. At the waist was a 4 or 5 inch pleated yellow cummerbund. The bodice of satin was also covered with the pale yellow organdy and gathered to a jewel neckline. Best of all, covering my thin arms were bouffant sleeves of the pale transparent organdy which were caught at the wrists with circlets of yellow satin and also covered with the tiny bouquets of flowers.

I remember the prom. As we entered the gym I saw the ceiling fluttering with blue and yellow (our school colors) streamers and balloons. I remember hearing the band playing our favorite songs. I remember the fragrance of the single gardenia on my shoulder. But most of all, I remember my mother's gift of love.

It was the only prom I ever attended. Because of a serious illness I didn't attend my senior year of high school, or my senior prom.

Owed to June

Buy gifts for Dad, the bride and scholar,
Replace the faded flag,
Happy gifts to buy they all are,
But make my checkbook sag.

Adventures in Eating

There are very few of my buttery thumb prints on the pages of my big, blue copy of The Joy of Cooking. It must have been a gift. For me, the joy of cooking was to get the most nutritious foods from boxes, bottles and canisters into our mouths with the least effort. Maybe that's why I was intrigued by the big TACO BELL sign I saw above a fast food restaurant shortly after we moved to California. What's a tayco, I thought. I went inside and ordered a tayco. The clerk asked, "Do you want shredded or ground beef on your taco?" Then and there, I fell in love with Mexican food; nutritious, fast, tasty and cheap. This was a food adventure, but not my first.

We'd moved from the mountains and hills of Western Pennsylvania to the mainly flat terrain of Dayton, Ohio. While still unpacking, a new neighbor called to say she would bring a mango casserole over in half an hour. Of course, any food I didn't have to cook was welcome, but mangos? I split the tape of a box of books and pulled out the dictionary to look up mangos. To my delight I found that mangos are not only a tropical fruit, but in certain parts of the Midwest, green peppers. The steaming fragrant casserole of stuffed green peppers she brought is still a delicious memory.

I learned another new food word when living in Ohio. While searching the Sears catalog for children's corduroy pants, the colors listed were lemon, raspberry, and avocado. Okay, I thought, lemon is yellow, raspberry is red, but what color is avocado? Back to the dictionary. I found that avocados are green. I know a lot more about delicious avocados now.

I tried to make good tasting meals for our young children because I knew they'd be hungry in an hour if dinner was not satisfying. One night I watched my six-year-old scrub her peas under a lettuce leaf on her plate and admonished, "Stop playing with your food." Hmmm, I thought, maybe that's the answer. So began my theme meals. We had stick meals, ball meals, green meals, and orange meals to list a few. The stick meal was celery sticks, fish sticks, French fries, and popsicles. The ball meal was radishes, tater tots (potato balls), meat balls, and previously made and frozen balls of ice cream. The green meal was cream cheese with chives in stalks of celery, broccoli spears, green mashed potatoes, (a few drops of food color) and those stuffed green mangos, with pistachio ice cream for dessert. There was also the orange meal, orange wedges, orange chicken, steamed carrots, and orange sherbet. I also made Rainbow Soup, with help from a recipe in Highlights, a children's magazine. It was mostly frozen mixed vegetables in a rich broth, served with oyster crackers and rainbow sherbet.

But my favorite adventure in eating occurred in Denver, Colorado when my oldest daughter was a toddler. She sat between my husband and me in a perilously flimsy car seat slung over the back of the front seat. We stopped for ice cream and got her a tiny cone. She looked at it curiously, tasted it, and, with delight, promptly devoured it. She quickly learned to love those little ice cream cones. I still remember seeing those tiny fingers fly toward the welcome treat. Never did so little money buy such joy of eating.

Half a Bubble Out of Plumb

It's uncanny, but all my special occasions, like weddings, anniversaries, births, and graduations take place when my frequent flyer miles are blocked. Another thing, if I plan to take advantage of an Early Bird Dinner, I get there half an hour too soon or ten minutes too late.

I faithfully clip those coupon specials from the Sunday ads, and the Penny Saver because of my frugal nature. Trouble is, all too often when I show them to the clerk she says "Lady, this coupon expired 6 months ago." It's embarrassing.

Every time I open my new refrigerator, I know I bought it about a year ago, I remind myself to fill out the warranty card and send it in. Problem is, the card is safely stored, but I don't remember where. I just hope to find it and send it in before the refrigerator quits.

Recently I took the car for an oil change. As I pulled up to the bay I dug around for the discount coupon I was sure I had saved. The attendant, clipboard in hand, cleared his throat and said "You were just in here 6 weeks ago. You aren't really due for an oil change."

Debit cards, on- line banking, ATMs are all quite beyond me. The only PIN I'm at home with is a safety pin. I do use my credit card to pay for some things, like dinner out. I remember to double the tax, plus some and leave cash on the table. I was told the server doesn't have to report it as income that way. I also remember to cross out the tip line when paying the bill.

I may be half a bubble out of plumb, but only HALF.

Pills

I think the color of pills should reflect their use. For instance, heart pills should be apple red. Sticky heart valves might perk up to see bright red flowing through them. Anti-depressant pills could be a soft, sunny yellow gel. For a touch of humor, diuretic pills could be pea green. High blood pressure pills, so often a must, could be assorted bright, jelly bean colors to relieve the daily monotony. Stomach pills could be a soothing, not hot, pink, and calcium supplements a shiny, pearly white. I think pain pills should be available in a variety of colors, so that one could choose a favorite color for relief.

Lastly, to save money, those famous little blue pills men take could be colorless. Guys don't care what color they are as long as they work.

July

Hot dogs, corn dogs,
Potato chips and Fritos,
Party on at picnics,
But block sun and mosquitoes.

Exercising

When my doctor asked if I exercise several times a week, I said, "Yes." And I do... I exercise caution when going through barely yellow lights at intersections. I exercise tact when I do not tell my friend how awful the new haircut looks. I exercise generosity when I give my grandchild my share of broccoli. I exercise patience when I mislay the mailbox key for the third time this week and must search for it. I exercise frugality when I go out for the early bird special instead of dining later. I exercise politeness when I give up my time on the treadmill to the person waiting to use it. I exercise bravery when I promise to host next year's Thanksgiving dinner for my children and grandchildren. I exercise concern when I turn up at the party without the dish I promised to bring.

Finally, just yesterday my accident prone neighbor asked if I wanted a ride to the store. I said, "No thanks, I'll walk. I need the exercise."

Getting the Job Done

My mother said, "Put an egg in the bowl and beat it." I put the egg in the bowl and left the kitchen. My sister thought that was funny, I did too. My mother did not.

Sometimes getting the job done is an art. Not until I put the bowl of jello and hot water on a bright pot holder and said, "Now stir until you can see the rooster clearly," did I get jello properly made by my reluctant child helper. I also used to line up peanut butter, white sandwich bread, cocktail toothpicks, raisins, and sprinkles and suggest the children make peanut butterflies. It took them quite some time to realize they were making their own lunches.

Dressing my toddler daughter full of "Nos" was not fun, until I asked her if she wanted to play Little Red Riding Hood. She said "Yes." I said, "Find me a red shirt, some red pants, and two red sox." She wore a lot of red that year but it got the job done. It worked with Little Boy Blue, too.

But by far my greatest helper in getting the job done was my kitchen timer. As I turned the timer on, I'd say, "When the timer dings, make your bed, unload the dishwasher take out the garbage," etc. The timer was the tyrant, not me. I remember so well seeing my oldest son look up from the cards he was shuffling, and saying, "We have time for one more game before the timer dings."

Nearby, I wiggled my toes on the comfy hassock, sipped a fizzy coke and turned the page of my magazine.

Stubborn

Good genes, favorable environment, luck and a healthy lifestyle have a lot to do with it, but I think those of us who have lived long beyond the pangs and passions of youth have a strong streak of stubbornness.

I must have been a stubborn kid. My father, not unkindly, called me "a square-headed Dutchman (German)," though I am solidly half Irish. I guess I usually got whatever I seriously determined to have.

My own first recollection of stubbornness was when, at about age 6 or 7, my father brought home a pair of roller skates for me. I eyed them critically, noting the soft leather panel which laced over the arch of the foot, and said, "Those are baby skates. I want skates with ball 'bearians.'" He tried, with no success, to explain that my feet were too small for skates with ball bearings. He, a machinist, finally bought and cut down steel skates which did fit my feet. I wore them for more than five years, and he patiently extended the axle and replaced the wheels when the steel wore through and the ball bearings fell out.

Stubbornness can save money. A collection of readings was a required text for a sophomore course in Comparative Literature. At the bookstore I discovered that the text was expensive, heavy and had fine print on tissue thin pages. I didn't buy it. Instead, each week I went to the library and looked up the readings. Very often, I found the library selection was lighter, had better print format and often included illustrations.

Stubbornness can call up unexpected bravery. Newcomers to California, we had just bought our ten-passenger station wagon. I commented that I had to take the driver's test and was apprehensive about parallel parking. The salesman said, "You can borrow my Mustang; it will be easier." "No thanks, I can do it," I said. Amazingly, I did.

I once stubbornly battled and won at "bait and switch." A department store nearby, in a full-page newspaper ad, offered a Boston rocker at a great price. Within an hour of the store's opening, I went there to buy the rocker. Brushing off the salesperson's attempt to steer me to a more expensive rocker, I asked for the manager, presented my case, and six weeks later got my Boston rocker. It's still in the family.

I confess I almost gave up on cream puffs. I dumped one dozen eggs into my Sunbeam Mixmaster, turned it on, and in a minute looked at uncooked, curdled, scrambled eggs. The "batter" looked so bad I threw the whole mess out. "This recipe is supposed to work," I mulled.

I must have done something wrong. I again put twelve eggs in the bowl, got to the curdled mess stage again, but kept mixing and folding just another two or three minutes and the "mess" turned into a mass of satiny batter. Despite calories and cholesterol, I still occasionally make picture-perfect cream puffs.

I'm a pretty good gardener, so when the nursery said fuchsias are difficult to grow in this hot, dry climate I thought, "Watch me." In my old yard in the San Francisco Bay Area I had big fuchsias, little fuchsias, fuchsias tall and fuchsias small on the fence and on the wall. So I bought them here. I planted them inside, outside always in shady spots. But as soon as I turned my back, my beauties drooped and threatened to die until I finally gave up. I failed fuchsias. But would you like a cream puff?

August

Hot, hotter, hottest,
I guess it must be August,
I think I'll stay inside
Till the calendar's un-fried.

My Grandmother's Sewing Machine

Doing our young family's mending was no problem. My mother's fancy electric sewing machine with the handy knee pedal was only minutes away. Getting the mending done became a much larger problem when we moved 300 miles east. On a visit home my Grandmother, who lived nearby, said, "You can have my old treadle machine if you want it." "I do, I do!" and it went home with us.

The machine looked bad. The lacy wrought iron frame holding the treadle and supporting the scarred compartment containing the lift-out sewing unit needed immediate attention because the only place I could put it was in the living room. First, I painted the wrought iron and treadle bright gold (maybe I was thinking of the evil gnome, Rumplstiltskin, who wove straw into gold at a huge price for the hapless princess). Next I put one of my grandmother's beautifully crocheted doilies (if you're feeling fiendish, ask anybody under twenty what a doily is). Next I bought an 18" tall hurricane lamp at a garage sale and put fake oil in the reservoir with the aid of yellow food color.

The sewing machine worked just fine. In fact on one memorable occasion it worked too well. It was Christmas Eve day and I was checking our clothes for Midnight Mass. In the deep pocket of the trousers of my husband's only suit, I found a big hole. I can fix that in a jiffy, I thought. I put the hurricane lamp and the doily on the dining room table and opened the hinged machine cabinet lid which formed a platform on which to put the garment to be sewn. All went well until I sewed the fleshy tip of my forefinger. Aghast, I tried to pull the broken needle out of my finger by tugging on the piece of thread. It would not budge. "I sewed my finger," I told my husband, "and I can't get the needle out." Off we went to the hospital on Christmas Eve.

As I lay there on the operating table, my left arm on a long swivel paddle extended from the table, I said, "This is ridiculous." On the wall was an x-ray of my finger, the piece of needle clearly visible, the thread still dangling from it. "No," the doctor said, "If the needle turns it could travel and stop your heart." The needle was successfully removed and only a small white scar reminds me of the incident.

I used the sewing machine three more years, admittedly a little more carefully. Finally, then we could afford an electric machine. Even now, many years later, I have strong legs, and, if I do say so myself, rather well turned ankles. I think I owe it all to my grandmother's treadle sewing machine.

Handicaps

My first big handicap was my younger sister. Everywhere I went I had to take her with me because our mother was not healthy. My sister wasn't a bad kid, she was just incessantly there. In vain I would try to slip out of bed and into a sun suit to go on an errand with my father. Inevitably though, I would turn around, to hear her ask as she tied her shoes, "Where are we going?" Finally, school released me from sister sitting most of the time.

Gym class at school was a second handicap. I was fast, but not strong. If I ever hit the baseball, I could beat the throw to first base. Usually though, I just struck out. Rainy days were good because we had gym class in the cavernous gymnasium. A fat rope, with a huge knot at the bottom, was secured to the high ceiling. I would jump up on the knot and easily scamper to the top and touch the roof. This got me coveted points in the grade book. I would pause; look down at the blue gym suited girls with great satisfaction, before descending.

Size can be a handicap. Once my mother brought home a blue and pink raincoat which was at least three or four sizes too big. Dismayed, she said, "It was on sale and I can't return it." Often I got soaked rather than wear the raincoat and never did grow into it.

Size is not always a handicap. When I try to reach something on a high shelf in the aisle of the super market, often someone will ask "Can I get that for you?" If no one is around to help, I remove an item or two from the bottom shelf and use the space as a stool to reach things over my head.

Once a good friend and I had a discussion about size as a handicap while we were eating our crackers and cheese in her office. We both felt our size was an asset. She, a commanding six feet tall, thought she got her way, sometimes undeservedly, because she looked imposing. We both laughed when I told her I thought I often got my way because people didn't expect much from a five foot puny person.

Some handicaps are obvious and must be dealt with. Some handicaps are hidden deep in the mind or body. Either way, I guess we just must learn to live with them and hope others lend a hand when we need it.

Summer Heat

The umbrella's up,
The chips are down,
Bring on the guacamole,
A bit of shade, cool drinks and food,
Will certainly console me.

A State of Mind

I bit down on the fresh pine clothes pins to keep my teeth from chattering as I pinned the last shirt to the clothes line on that cold January day just outside Denver, Colorado. The "Mile High City" ranked low on my pleasure scale. Yes, I did see President Dwight D. Eisenhower leave Fitzsimmons Army Hospital because I happened to be there for a check up. Yes I did stand astride the Continental Divide high in the Rocky Mountains. And indeed, the trout pulled from the clear, cold streams and grilled within the hour were the best I ever tasted. Still after Denver's thin, high dry air, I felt better the moment the plane lifted and headed back to what some westerners called "the sloppy wet east."

East was to New Jersey. What a pleasant shock it was to pay only the marked price for an item because New Jersey had no sales tax. Also, once you left the belching industrial and chemical plants around northern New Jersey, much of the so called "Garden State" was (and is) beautiful. I found many of New Jersey's names of cities and towns quaint, like Perth Amboy, Little Silver, and Metuchen. I loved classical music radio station WQXR out of New York, and WVNJ which played non-stop Broadway show songs. In a few years we headed west again, but only as far as Ohio.

Ohio must mean "friendly" in some language. We were deluged with welcome to the neighborhood casseroles, and invited to all sorts of clubs and social groups. Ohioans spend a lot of time indoors. I quickly discovered the reason. It was hot and humid in summer, freezing and overcast in winter and, worst of all, tornado prone. In a small city near us a tornado took the roof off a suburban home. A news photo showed toy soldiers still standing on the floor of a roofless bedroom. It was somewhat embarrassing when our wonderful neighbors staged a farewell block party for us. I still feel guilty about not liking Ohio.

Our next stop was Florida, "The Sunshine State." And it truly was. Trouble was, every kind of bug knew it too. Many summer nights one of the children would yell, "Close the windows! The fogger's coming down our street." It was the mosquito control truck and did help reduce mosquitoes. What the pesticide did or is still doing to our bodies is unknown to me. One late night at Jacksonville airport I watched as a huge cockroach lazily strolled up the suitcase beside me. I loved 80 degree Christmases, pecan pie, Indian River grapefruit, and romantic live oak trees draped in languidly swinging Spanish moss. Later I learned that Spanish Moss could destroy trees. Often I tuned into the University of Florida's radio program called "The Florida Gardner." I think that's where I learned the term "Yankee Hurricane," which is a hurricane that goes north then turns around and hits you. One late fall I looked up to see the tall loblolly pines twirling in the wind and rain. The hurricane churned our asphalt street to black "slush," and the water flooded about one foot of our terrazzo bedroom floor, but did no real damage.

Last stop was California. When the phone company guy came to install the Wall phone in our kitchen he asked, "Where'd you move from?" "Florida," I said. "I thought you must be from the South from your accent." he replied. I told him I loved the soft southern drawl, but was born and raised in Pennsylvania. Later, a new neighbor asked, "Why did you leave Florida?" My almost instant reply was, "Because the only state better to live in than Florida is California." That was years ago. I haven't changed my mind.

It's a Fake!

I love fakes. If I could get them on and off, I'd have fake eyelashes. I wear a fake "diamond" necklace. If a mugger knocks me over and grabs it, I'll shout, if I'm able, "Ha! It's a fake."

My sterling silver flatware lies in its airtight box under a blanket of felt. I prefer stainless steel "silverware" that goes from table to mouth to dishwasher and back again without pampering.

I like orchids, but can never remember whether to water them every eight days or every eight months. Real orchids look like fakes, so why not buy fakes in the first place? Dust them once a month and you're done.

I use imitation vanilla in my recipes. I once priced a real vanilla bean and immediately lost my appetite. Purists might disagree, but imitation crab in my hot crab hors d'oeuvres tastes good to me.

I love faux fur – can't afford the real thing anyway. I do confess I own a rabbit fur jacket, but I don't feel this is a major transgression.

Even fake accents in old movies don't bother me. But it had better be a three star movie. At least.

Little Big Decisions

Life's big decisions are usually made after careful consideration. For instance, deciding which school to attend, who to marry, which state to live in or how many children to have. But there are a lot of what I call 'little big decisions' along the way. They begin early.

When I was about seven, my dad asked, "Do you want an orange drink or an Eskimo Pie?" It was a sticky, hot July day in western Pennsylvania, so the decision was not an easy one. Not too long after that, I tried to check out six books and the librarian said, "You may have only four books." Another decision. Hmmm, should I put back two Louisa May Alcott books or two Grimm's fairy tale books, or one of each? In junior high, the counselor said, "You can be on my student cabinet or on the student court, but not both." Another prickly choice.

And the little big decisions didn't stop. Did I want to spend my babysitting money on streetcar fare downtown to see a newly released movie at an air conditioned theater, or see three older movies locally? Did I want prescription sunglasses or a new dress for graduation? As a young professional, did I want good looking basic beige pumps, or the red stiletto-heeled sandals I really craved? Did I want a big car with no frills, or a small car with many?

I have decided there is no relief from making little big decisions. Right now, do I want a big handful of delicious, sun-dried apricots, or a very small hot fudge sundae with crushed nuts, whipped cream and a maraschino cherry? Yeah, you guessed it.

September Sermon

Resolutions cast aside,
The days turned into months I cried!
The year has now begun its slide,
Relax....enjoy the ride.

Picky People

My children tell me I'm picky, but I'm not. I did not raise picky children either. Generally, they wore the clothes I chose, skirt lengths and jeans styles were somewhat negotiable. They drank mainly water, 2% milk or Kool Aid, and ate whatever I put on the table. None of them had to eat unusual foods like sauerkraut or cabbage rolls.

That's why I'm puzzled now when my children tell me that I'm picky. I do have a few minor preferences. I will not sneeze in a house without Puffs. When you pull a Kleenex, you may get one, but you may get two or three. Not so with Puffs. You get one every time. Also, I like my coffee with half and half, not black, not sugared, not flavored and never with pure cream. Another thing, when I go for a ride, I carry my own car pillow. Fine upholstery, buttery leather or even heated seats don't impress me. My car pillow, though a bit faded, a little frayed at the seams, and with a few small coffee stains still gives me the most comfortable ride.

My son and his wife invited me for dinner recently. He knows I like a martini before dinner. Once he made me a martini with fancy French vermouth which tasted all wrong. Now he knows to keep my favorite California extra dry vermouth on hand. Incidentally, a martini is always made with gin, never vodka.

When my children invite me for dinner and ask what I'd like, I tell them, "I'm not picky, I eat everything." They do know that although I like meat, I like it covered with something, anything so that I'm not really aware that it is meat I'm eating. Also, it must be boneless. Bones belong under the skin, never on my plate. As for vegetables, neither crisp nor mushy will do. Fork tender and hot is the only way to eat vegetables.

So here I am at the computer. I glance at my desk calendar to my left. There is nothing scheduled, but doctor and hair appointments, and a smoke alarm inspection. My coffee mugs are ready, in case someone stops by, all of them facing right, of course. My car pillow is nearby. I hope somebody comes to visit, or calls to invite me to go for a ride. Either one. I'm not picky.

Remotes...or What's In a Name?

I sit here in the living room fanning my remotes. There are seven. Do I want news or a sitcom on TV? An old movie on the VCR? A new movie on the DVD? Or just music on the radio or stereo? I've worked up a sweat just deciding, so I finger the ceiling fan remote to possibly seek relief. When did "remote" become a noun anyway? It used to be an adjective, as in, "I don't have the remotest idea where you left your car keys." Occasionally I'd use the adverb, as in, "I remotely remember failing to record that purchase in the check register."

Once the TV remote failed and I actually had to walk to the TV to turn it on. I stuck my finger through a cobweb to do it. And since when do we turn on anything. All I seem to turn these days is a pancake, a bottle cap or over in bed.

I've learned a lot about batteries since I acquired these electronic marvels. We used to keep mostly Cs or Ds around to make flashlights light, the velvet Santa dance or Chatty Cathy talk. Now I have a world class supply of batteries, triple A, double A, nine volt, rechargeable and lithium. I have a battery checker and, just in case, a backup battery checker. A frugal person, I also have a battery charger; to be honest, I have two of them.

Once in a while I hear a remote called a "clicker." Ridiculous! A remote makes no noise; it just carries out its work quietly. I might call it a magic wand, but NEVER a "clicker." Somebody ought to write a song about remotes. Maybe something like, "The Sounds of Silence II," fully orchestrated, of course.

Anchors Away

I flicked on the living room TV and upped the volume so I could hear the news as I unloaded the dishwasher in the kitchen. I heard "Hey, Patsy," then "Hey, Fred." I rushed around the corner to see what had befallen Fred and Patsy. Turns out they were just greeting each other. When did "hey" replace "hi," or "hello" as a greeting?

I pause to look at them. Fred, (short for Fredrika) is a gorgeous redhead, and Patsy is a tall, dark and handsome male. When did these chiseled chaps and charming chirpies replace Edward R. Murrow and Walter Cronkite, who just gave us the facts like Sgt. Joe Friday did on *Dragnet*?

Fred turns from Patsy, looks at me and says, "Hey, everybody, here's the top story...." She loses me. I'm not 'everybody,' I'm just me. Here alone in my living room. Besides, I can't really concentrate on what she is saying. I'm too busy looking at her sculptured red sheath of hair cupping white ear lobes, from which hang fascinating earrings. I try to guess: Tiffany? Cartier? Wal-Mart? Patsy gives me trouble, too. He keeps flicking his designer glasses on and off. Why can't he succumb to bifocals, wear contact lenses, or enlarge the font on the TelePrompTer? Frankly, I'm beginning to suspect the glasses are just a prop to keep my attention.

Both anchors sit at a desk so I can't be sure about their footwear, but I'm guessing she's sporting Manolo Blahnik heels and he's shod in Italian Bruno Maglis. Both about $400 a pair. Anchors make a lot of money. I know because I heard it on the radio or read it in the newspaper.

Next Fred smoothes her already sleek hair and looks at Patsy. He pockets his glasses and says, "And now for a weather update." They both look left and the Weather Waif appears. I fear a slight breeze will sweep her off the set. Her name is Stormy.

Disgusted, I snap off the TV. Two minutes later I can still see the glow of their perfect white teeth on the blank screen.

October

Summer's heat was yesterday,
Holidays, still far away,
October sweet upon the scene,
Delightful season in between.

Great Expectations

Rain is predicted for tomorrow. I must shed the languor of months of dry sun baked days and prepare for its arrival. The tools carelessly left on the glider, on the top of the storage unit and on the hose reel frame must be properly stored. I survey my little landscape and act.

I pull the feathery asparagus fern through the wrought iron fence and direct it around the base of the big fountain. Then I notice the nearby bright green, but frail, leaves of the mock orange bush mask dead wood lurking beneath. I prune it heartlessly to promote fresh growth.

Next I pound my slim shaft of sturdy rebar into the super dry soil under the trees and bushes so that every precious drop of moisture gets to the thirsty roots. I also clear the area of old bark, yellowed needles, and dropped eucalyptus leaves to be sure no rain is wasted.

The wide ledges under the dining room window and the narrow ledges under the bay window in the kitchen must be dusted with my big blue soft bristled brush to prevent the rain from streaking the freshly painted stucco.

I glance up at the gathering clouds and see that the gutters will have to be cleared after the rain to prevent roof dust from washing into them and both curtailing runoff and causing damage.

I think I'm done. The waste bin is full. To my delight, the nimbus clouds release their nectar. Rain falls. I hear it on the skylights. I resist the urge to throw down a red and white tablecloth and get out ketchup and mustard. The rain is here. All hail the rain.

The Economy

The winners in November will be the ones who listen to me now. This is my platform.

All Medicare card-carrying citizens will have hair care, foot care and nail care covered by their insurance, with no co-pay. I don't mean haircuts at the chop shop down the block or minimal clip-and-skip toenail cutting in an antiseptic, cold doctor's cubicle.

First, here's how hair care should work. I go to my favorite stylist, who attacks my rather challenging hair free of charge after I flash my Medicare card. I look so much better that I bounce out of the salon and write checks to all my grandchildren for a blowout trip to the mall. This stimulates the economy.

When I show my Medicare card to the receptionist at the nail care spa, she sees to it that I am immediately seen by a manicurist. In an hour my nails look so good I decide I must replace my garden gloves and, since I'll be on my knees, I need sturdy clogs and tough pants. While I'm outside, I see that several plants need to be replaced and some suspicious looking posts need to be checked for dry rot. Getting my nails done leads to a trip to several stores – for supplies, a trip to the garden center to buy replacement plants, and then I'll probably need someone to replace the patio cover. This all stimulates the economy.

I'm promoting a Medicare pedicure. I could read a glossy magazine and sip a juice drink while I soak my feet in a whirlpool bath. I'd feel so energized after this treatment that I'd walk all over, visiting many stores and exercising my credit card to the max because my feet were so comfy. My purchases would boost the economy.

I feel so healthy and look so good I decide to try a new restaurant, pausing only to call three friends to join me. They enjoy their meal so much that they call their families about the new restaurant. I'm quite sure this would create more than a few jobs. Again, this spikes the economy.

Networks will call, cable news will be interested. They want to engage me as a political analyst. I intend to tell them it's a possibility – if I can fit them into my busy schedule.

The Right Stuff

Each November the grocery ads offer about the same items needed to prepare the big Thanksgiving Day dinner. But for several years now I have noticed an unfamiliar item. Stuffing mix. Wait a minute! You don't BUY stuffing mix, you MAKE stuffing mix. First you toast about a loaf of sliced white sandwich bread and cut each slice into quarter inch cubes. Next, in a large skillet, sauté in butter diced yellow onion, chopped celery, and add spices. Last, add the bread cubes and simmer a few minutes, then fill the turkey with the mixture. At no time do you add such foreign objects as sausage, nuts, or corn bread. Now THAT'S the right stuff.

Christmas Treats

If, as Nat King Cole sang, chestnuts were roasting on an open fire, the Neighborhood Watch would be at my door swiftly followed by The Fire Dept. But who would want to do that anyway? The only chestnuts I've seen are shiny brown marble size things that threaten to break a dental crown just looking at them. Furthermore, I love his song, but I'll bet Nat King Cole never roasted chestnuts on an open fire either.

Remember the line in "Twas the Night before Christmas," where children see visions of sugar plums dance in their heads? I looked it up and sugar plums are not plums at all; they're small hard candies. If visions of anything are dancing in children's heads, it's probably a reflection of their digital camera trying for a first ever picture of Santa Claus exiting a fat bumpy cloud with the next kid video special in his bag.

Speaking of Christmas Treats, does anyone ever eat mincemeat pie? You really don't want to know what is in mincemeat pie. Same thing with Christmas fruit cakes. I don't know what is in them and I am NEVER going to find out.

Here's my recipe for a Christmas Treat. Skip eating chestnuts, sugar plums, mincemeat pie, and fruit cake. Try drinking eggnog. If it doesn't taste good plain, add some alcohol, keep adding alcohol until you are happy. Cheers.

Aloha

After thirty years of family Christmases I decided to fly to Hawaii on Christmas Day. It was an unusually cold December in the Bay Area. Our friend, a manager of an apartment building in Palo Alto had to rush back, after dropping us off at the airport because some water pipes had burst.

The plane was half full and very quiet. Landing preparations joggled me awake just in time to see us land amid the black lava at Kona International Airport at Keahole on the Big Island of Hawaii.

I ran to the restroom and changed into a tank top and shorts which I'd put in my carry-on, then picked up our luggage and waited while my sister arranged for our rental car. To pass the time I opened the box of See's candy I'd bought at San Francisco International Airport, carefully eating the nut clusters and leaving the chews for my sister.

I bought some Christmas cards at an ABC store and sat down on the lanai of our high hotel to address them. Almost all started with "Sorry this is late but...." I later discovered that those Christmas cards with Poinsettias as high as rooftops were not only an artist's rendition, but actually existed all over the island.

One memorable day we sat on a black sand beach and then later the same day stood on a pulsing lava plain, part of which would be no more within the year when Kilauea volcano erupted.

When the lights of the San Francisco Bay Area appeared in the window of the plane on our return trip home, I breathed, "Aloha." I had just learned that Aloha means both "hello," and "good-bye."

December Wrap Up

I've worked and played,
Achieved and prayed,
And now the year must end,
Thoughts drive me to wonder,
What's around the bend?